jam alerts

linh dinh

chax press

2007

ISBN 978-0-925904-68-3

Produced in the United States of America
Chax Press / 101 W. Sixth St. / Tucson Arizona 85701-1000
http://www.chax.org

Poems in *Jam Alerts* have been published in *Effing, Fourteen Hills, Great Works, Green Integer Review, Mipoesias, Ocho, Quarterly West, Tantalum* and *West Wind Review.* Two poems were translated into Portuguese and published in *Sibila.* A selection was released as a chapbook in England, *I Haven't Been Anywhere, Man* (Norwich: Landfill Press, 2007).

I would like to thank Mr. David T.K. Wong, the University of East Anglia and the Lannan Foundation, for providing me time to write much of this book.

Table of Contents

Getting Up Conditional

Munching something fingers, we fled
From one barf fest to the next. After
Much yawping, we finally arrived

Inside the chunnel for the money shot.
It's not a misfortune, really, to be born
Ass backward in a cul-de-sac. Once

I turned down a predatory gift from one
Who could least afford it. Straddling
A squishy balloon, erect, she peeled

Old calk from an ancient calk gun.
No more mirth until tomorrow, at least.

Brief Biographies

Short of all vitamins and calcium, malformed,
My mom a yawning question mark, I wasn't born
From a warmed egg, but sculpted from the surfeit
Of a bombastic masturbator, clouding a bathtub.
Raised on no milk, I sucked and suckled myself
Into this laughing pretension.

*

The least and last of 99 roll-outs, 98 of them
Troglodytes or shuffling sideways, I was bred
With a colorful xerox of my mama's mammae,
Muzak and a printout of my pop's corny digits.
Now I huff after ingots and a synapse-born shine
That doesn't even translate into adjacent dialects,
To be erased, in any case, with the next martini
Or rickshaw mishap.

*

You've heard this one: a predictable punch line
To all jokes, I'm the bug in that cheesy proverb.
On the other hand, it's also nice to have sinews,
I'm testing my equipments.

Who braised you?

So anyway, the hogs were out bawling,
The limp tongue chided the snide tooth,
And all were sweating to be naked
Once more, before being upgraded for
The years-end liquidation, the rapture,
Or something like that.

The Persistence of Animism

Born-again death row inmate confides to his rectangle
Of cracked concrete. A groom chit chats with his mare,
Daring it to lick his soiled face. Cruising to rock towards
Another crunchy pileup, modern man has prolonged sex
With his cozy, steely host, baptizes it with a wet phrase.

Tagging

He'd refer to the same structure as a hut
One day, a gazebo the next, sometimes
As an estate, a villa or a dacha. His voice
Lowered, he'd mention it as a compound.

Although we've known each others for decades,
He calls me by a different name each time. I would
Suddenly become a Theo, a Frank or a Mohammad.
You look like a Mohammad today, he'd explain.

He even tags his wife diversely. I suspect he genuinely
Believes she's a different person each time he glances
At her across the dinner table, or in the semi darkness
After their rote, shabby and indeterminate lovemaking.

How to Walk

Many people firmly believe that to walk properly, one must
Square one's shoulders, straighten one's spine and steer
All of one's toes resolutely forward. It is ill-advised
To keep hands in pockets—especially one hand
In one pocket. They are contemptuous
Of all those who waddle, sidle, glide, sashay,
Cake walk or, God forbid, walk backward.

Call me disturbed, if you will, but I've been haunted,
For decades, by how folks propel themselves forward
In Malevich's paintings. Most trudge, stiff legged,
Their bodies impossible. Some parade,
But singly, their hands swimming,
Their boneless arms flapping.

Seriously gorgeous, to have a bod above ground
Is gravy, mostly, creeping or crawling, but is there
No rest for the green man?

I Paid for Sex!

Well, who doesn't? Let's examine this naked man,
Struck and killed today, just west of Snoqualmie Pass.
The owner of three McDonald's in Ellensburg. Around 4 AM,
He was driving a red pickup on I-90 when it crossed the median,
Coming to a stop when it struck a guardrail. He exited his truck,
Took off his clothes and stood in the eastbound lanes, where
He was struck by a white pickup of someone going to work.

Investigators have no idea why this man removed his clothing.
Temperatures at the pass hovered around freezing at daybreak.

Adding to the mystery, a dead dog was found nearby, its carcass
Straddled two eastbound lanes, nearest the shoulder.

Jam Alerts

5:13 AM, FATL HIT N RUN, SUSP FLEEING, ARTERIES CLGGD.

5:47 AM, JAM ALERT, DBRIS, CHUNKS, SUVS, SOCCR MOMS.

6:34 AM, SAND NEEDED FOR OIL, BLD SPLLS ACRSS ALL LANES.

6:39 AM, STRUCTURE, CORRCTN, STRUCTURAL FCKUPS, MJR.

7:05 AM, POSSBL RIOT, XPLSIONS HRD, FLG POLE KNCKD OFF BSE.

7:50 AM, POLICE N MERGNCY CRW ATTCKD BY OUTRGD NATIVS.

8:15 AM, RTS DIVERTD, TNKS, HOT CHEERLEADRS, HIYA, PARADE.

8:22 AM, WHITE HSE PORCH TORCHD, PRESDNTL PRESS CONFER.

8:58 AM, EL CAMINO REAL RENAMD EL REALLY FCKIN LONG MRCH.

9:01 AM, PNTGN RENAMD FLL SPCTRUM WRLD PCE KEEPNG AGNCY.

9:02 AM, DOMINOS COLLPSNG FR REAL, VEHS OVRTURND, BURNNG.

9:03 AM, MOB STRMS WHITE HSE, HNGS PRS BUSH UPSDE DOWN.

9:18 AM, WET DRM, NSTLGIA NSCAR RCE IN EMPTY PRKG LOT.

9:46 AM, WTR OUT, BRD N MLK OUT, PLSTC FLGS APLENTY.

Celebration

When this bullshit
Word edifice burns,
It means your mouth's
Decomposing.

Not enough—seven times
In Disneyland, and that's
Just this week, alone.

Always piss outside, save water.
Step off the pavement and drizzle
On the first patch of grass you see.

Abort yourself
For the planet.

Too Late Late Capitalism

A plate of free-ranging eggs, fried with palm oil,
On a plastic chaise lounge—how poetic is that?
I'd never settle for polyester, spandex or rayon
For my goddess, free-ranging daughters. Where
Did all that money and sex go? (They drained
Down your bottomless bell bottoms, of course.)
I don't get why folks bother with chicken wings?
There's no meat on them. Totally tuckered from
Working out on a Solid Pecs Flab Burning Rack,
I chill with Whitman on my billion blades of grass.

Addendum: this farmers' market's a chain.
The ships are gone, the chowder remains.

No Clues but in Things

A well-rounded man with a tank belly and a basin mouth said,
"Cast into this mirage, it behooves us to have swimming pools.
Each time I rinse my well-tucked assets, I need several lochs."

Exporting peanuts, the average Gambian uses 4.5 liters per day,
Less than 1/3 of what you and I flush down the toilet each time.
(Shoot, that's not even adequate to dab the corns on my nuts.)
Can I have my action man cool dude celebration twinkie now?
Can I have my all stars victory flavored champion cake now?

Though more expensive, a dug-in pool is the perfect medium
For you to space out in the privacy of your own lot—after all,
You're not just seizing comfort, you're charging your karma.

Behavin'

Living a full life without a square meal, crouching
Inside an oil drum teetering on a plastic niagara,
I dream of stitching winged goddesses of victory
For a cheekful of cashews and a kick in the ass.
Raising lobsters for the man, I go nether on hogs.

Ways to an EZier Life

Rims on your hot rod,
Whitening your fangs.
"You don't need cash,
To live richly. Just be
Honest with yourself."
"Yes, boss." In 2004,
The American CEO/
Worker pay ratio
Was 431 to one.

By early afternoon of new year's day,
Unseasonably warm, no polar bears,
This nation's top hogs have already
Made as much as the annual salary
Of minimum wage suckers, such as
My wife and your waddling mama.

$

On a day, in a world,
In which many people were stripped
Of their houses, spouses, children,
Countries, limbs, life and honor,
He was devastated after looking for hours
Without finding a dollar he had misplaced.
It's not the amount, it's the principle.

*

Money protects you against assholes,
A deep voice, redolent of roast beef, said,
While greasing you to become an asshole.

*

Money in the brain? Yes.
Money in the heart? Yes.
Money in the eyes? Yes.
Money in the mouth? Yes.
Money in the hands? Not sure.
Money in the belly? Sometimes.
Money in the dick? Difficult.
Money in the pussy? Sure thing.
Money in the asshole? Yes.

*

Money chops up all the tangible
And intangible things of this universe
Into equal, instantly understood units.

8 units of pasta equal one unit of roast beef.
10 units of roast beef equal one unit of pop music.
23 units of pop music equal one unit of laughable sex.
5 units of laughable sex equal one unit of good poetry.

*

He doesn't ask, Is this book any good?
But, Is this author any rich?

Some Moves

If you have never bought it here, you have probably
Always paid too much for it. It is always satisfactory—
Continuous effort on our part keeps it so. It's absolutely
An everyday-of-the-year product. We doubt if you can
Find such a product at this price anywhere but here.
Truly a price that defies competition and belief.
Try it and see! We speculate we may then count you
Among our most loyal & rabid customers. In short,
My eyes desire you above all things.

In Praise of Pimples

Ca-chink mirages, besieged and festooned by an ocean
Of parking, shopping malls are totalitarian. You are told
To do one thing and one thing only. There's no mishmash
Of architecture to betray history and place, no upper floors,
Balustrades, cornices, pediments, chimneys, birds and sky
For the eyes to soar and rest. At best, nature is canned there.
Packed into corporate boxes, these shops can show no pimples.

Ad Hoc Finitum

A frank stoner, it has a curt ceramic socket
Under a lanky iron plunger. With the chosen
Cherry in place, one abrupt stab cleanly evicts
The unfortunate stone.

With a rubber add-on and a fluid-filled vacuum
At its base, the bird chirps suddenly, grabbing
The drifting child's attention, so the gentleman
Could bag his philistine keepsake.

We also have neat drawers to stash your shavings,
And fingers that go in and out when under pressure.

Pricing Culture

The very rare poems that are worth anything
Are sold by the line, at 20 cents per. Rhymes,
Including internal or near, are extra, at 2 cents per.
Any startling image, surrealist or otherwise, usually
Bloody, sexual or just plain weird, are also extra,
At 2 cents per.

Paintings are valued by the square inch, at 10 dollars per,
With surcharges tagged on for expensive hues, including
Those derived from finite commodities, such as minerals:
Cobalt blue, zinc white and every cadmium color. Those
Extracted from relatively abundant, renewable resources
Such as Indian yellow, made from cow urine, are inclusive
In the quoted square inch price, although extra thick paint,
Such as common in many macho schools, will cost extra.

Public holdings of plastic arts can be glimpsed
In 30-second intervals, at 25 cents per. So-called
Masterpieces or unusually popular junk, Renoir,
For example, can be ogled at for a tad higher.

Box Shopping

Going Home, Horizon, Cruise,
Wayfarer, Ambassador, Sleep.

Material: 18-gauge steel.
Finish: Brushed copper with Roman bronze shading
Or Neapolitan blue with slightly tacky wavy patterns.
Design: Square, diagonal or round corners, gasketed.

THERE'S NO SCIENTIFIC OR OTHER EVIDENCE
THAT A MODEL WITH A SEALING DEVICE WILL
IMMORTALIZE YOUR MORTAL AGGREGATE.

Interior: Nude Crepe or Champagne Velvet.
Embroidered Mama theme head panel,
Stars and Stripes or Lady of Guadalupe.
Silver or gold-colored fixed handles
With bright yet tasteful floral decals.

Adjustable mattress, of course,
With a vast selection of pillows
To choose from. Vanity models,
Lined with mirrors, also available.

Interior width at body sides: you.
Interior length at body sides: you.
Maximum weight: 240 lbs.
($14.99 each additional lb.)

Monterey, Carmel, Monte Carlo, Capri,
Cote d'Azur, Lethe, Plymouth Rock.
Deep discounts on showroom samples.
Overnight Delivery—Flexible Financing.

Live to Count

The Piraha people of Brazil can count only to 2.
Any number greater than 2—3 or a billion—
They only indicate as many.

Americans, on the other hand, love to count,
And can do it very accurately. Perhaps that's why
They have so many things and can ingest so many
Sedatives.

I, on the other hand, like to count corpses.

Whenever I see corpses, I always mumble 1, 2, 3, 4
5, 6, 7, 8, 9, 10, 11, 12, 13, 14, 15. When I don't see
Corpses, I count living people as corpses.

I'm always waiting for an opportunity to count corpses.
Perhaps I'm only here on this earth to count corpses.

When I meet someone, I'd ask, Are you dead yet?
Meeting an 89-year-old man, I'd say, Are you dead yet?
Seeing a relative, father, mother, aunt, uncle, cousin,
Child or grandchild, I'd interrogate, Are you dead yet?

Seeing an infant just born 2 or 3 minutes ago, I'd stare
Straight into its mother's eyes, Is your child dead yet?

Whenever I hear, Not yet, I'm always devastated,
Even bewildered. Are you sure? Why aren't you
Dead yet? Why won't you die already?

The Travel Stall

Moving through space to air out the psyche,
Travelling only works if done singly, of course,
And not en masse, as in a double-decker bus.
You should not aim to rush through a city,
A continent or the entire world, but to see
As clearly as possible a single spot, even if
It's that street corner in front of your house.

With this in mind, we have developed the Travel Stall.
The same size as a phone booth and completely lined
With one-way mirrors, the Travel Stall can be rented
By the hour, the day or even for a week, complete
With a sanitary bucket. Once entered, you cannot leave
Before the agreed-upon duration. With nothing to do
For 12 hours, for example, you'll be forced to examine
The universe in front of your eyes, as if for the first time.

Two or more Travel Stalls can be set up side by side,
To accommodate couples or families with children or pets.
Discounts available for seniors, students and veterans.

I Haven't Been Anywhere, Man

On November 3rd, 2005, the BBC published: "Vietnamese Boy
'Swam' to Beach." It's about a 14-year-old boy found freezing
On a Welsh beach. He had apparently fled his home country,
Jumped ship as it neared Swansea before swimming ashore.

On December 18th, 2005, the BBC published: "Farmer's Dream
Ends at Heathrow." It's about a Polish farmer who disappeared
From his native village, Znin, to be found wandering around
London's vast labyrinth of an airport, in search of a new life.

Ludwik Zon, 84, spent years pinching to raise $3,000 for his trip.
Without a word to his family, he donned his best clothes and rode
His bike to catch a bus and train to Warsaw, then flew to London.

While dozens of cops and firemen searched forests and fields
Around lovely Znin, hoping to find a chunk or two, Zon poked
Around Heathrow until the bobbies sent him home.

Back home, Zon said: "It's too bad I wasn't allowed to stay longer,
Because people there have got a wonderful life. I thought I might
Look about for a job. Here in Poland, a person hasn't got a future."

By the Navidad in 1830

A wild, two legged thing,
No naked white woman running,
An "it" that comes after midnight,
Right pass the sleeping hounds,
Into the kitchen to filch an apple,
Which you'll return later, the core.
Once you stole a novel and a bible,
Scrunched up their pages for wiping.
Lost child, hiding behind the yucca,
Or dozing on the flat fork of an oak,
Chewing arrowheads and cattails
When nothing else is reachable,
You crossed the ocean in chains
To this land of the free and home
Of the something or other, etc.

Demarcations

Frontière, frontiera, frontera,
Grenze, border, what separates
Also connects, crossing it always
Triggers an instant high, although

The geografia is exactly igual,
And la gente and arquitectura
Haven't changed all that much.

What do you have in that trunk, Sir?
A relative? Your girlfriend? Something
White? Two tons of it? Something green,
Like horseshit, after you've stepped on it?

Negotiated with blood, a boundary
Is nevertheless an illogical entity.
Standing on one side, staring across,
One can't comprehend why one isn't
Allowed to just pop over. If someone

Draws a line on the ground, and declares,
This is something you mustn't transgress,
The first impulse is to kick sand, naturally.

Yesterday, a naked man was spotted walking
Across the border, at its most exposed link.
Which way was he going? Does it matter?
Meanwhile, on the radio: muchacha,
Give me your cha cha!

Correspondence

An unwelcome guest,
Thriving along fences,
Round and tumbling,
It maintains its integrity
While dying, then later,
It scatters its offspring
Like a rambling stud.

Imitating the weed,
I wander this desert,
Seminating everything,
Coupling snakes, pigs,
Rats and scorpions.

Preliminary Questions

Don't ask, Where are you from? Inquire,
What time are you coming to the party?
I'll bring a bottle. Imported. Don't worry
About losing your tongue, I've already
Misplaced mine, along with a banana,
24k watch and who knows what else,
The last time you kindly dropped by
My beachfront property.

Why Pay Taxes?

You call it maize,
Hang it by Jesus.
I call it corn syrup.

Don't want no Blue Ox or Red Bull,
Just give me a tall bottle of fizzin',
Old fashioned, syrupy corn syrup.

Shurfine supposedly pork sausage,
Less than 99% corn syrup, exactly
The way I like it. Shurfine ketchup,
Approaching 200% corn syrup.

Subsidized by my 24/7 huffing and sweating,
Corn syrup oozes through my jiggling mass.
Sugar, let me rub some corn syrup on ya.

Canto LXI ½

China your good friend, her friendship spreads!
(Since reforms and door opens, China spreads.)
Where is the best source of protein? Adopting
Advanced equipment and manufactured finely,
The noodle is still flipping after being cooked.
With the natural seasoning, dried something,
Green vegetables and bone juice, the juice
Is pungent aftertaste, buzzing years hence.

Wide, smooth roads, acacia fraught ramps,
Orderly street lamps, quite lots of factories.
What is more, there are opera schools, art
And thespian working cells, brass sections,
Drum sets, croquet teams, culture gardens,
Medical shacks, libraries, healthful gardens,
Computer & math halls, millennium gardens,
Cracking kindergartens, schools, telecast
And newspaper hacks run by our Party.

All sworn members, cadres and villagers
Are urged to achieve diligent chumphood,
Sincere and helpful, each folds and tucks
Himself into a dank niche, gives and grins.
The superior cadres sing highly laudatives.

All subjects of this paradisal lot, the toddlers
Are carefully watched after, the kids are OK,
The slim, tackily-dressed young drip breezily
And the nearly dust are cheerfully disposed.

Wrong Countries

What constitute a wrong country? One
That's always lectured and bombed, or one

That cannot stop bombing? A wrong country
Cannot compete? In what? Founded on

A miscalculated philosophy, it is farcically
Hypocritical and hosannas, by examples,

All the sickest values. A wrong country has
Taken a wrong turn? Right from the start?

A wrong country maintains all of its subjects
In solitary confinement, all the time. You know

You're living in a wrong one when all you want
Is to decamp soon, or to burrow inside yourself

Until Armageddon, which will debut, you hope,
Before the next nightmare farce of an election.

Blue Passport Blues

Accident of geography and time, you've done nothing
To earn your fossil drain, your burning of huts, your
24-hour contact sports from sea to shining sea, your
Jazzy exhaust, marvelous freeway exchanges, sex
Vacations, roadside bombs and hacked elections.

Foddering Dollops

Unlike other corpses, these corpses
Can speak for themselves, perhaps.

Terrorized into heroism, they were blasted
Into the annals of the anal who had chosen
Not to participate.

Dead for a pipeline dream.

Rueful Outlays for a Conscript

Minus the moneyed, defective and ministers of religion,
What is left is sucked into the intake, paid some fraction
Of what they deserve, trained for a period of months,
Then spat out, in one piece or several, adding no value,
Really, no advantage to this high-tech peace machinery.

This churning that takes place requires
An enormous amount of effort in training,
And then they were gone...

No two-bit fruit-peeling racket,
No cookie monster slicer and sorter,
No depleted uranium sushi fridge,
No wine chiller with blinking canopy,
No spiral dough kneader and mixer,
No candy-assed gelato churner,
No, Sir, this is a real meat grinder.

Detonating Gamers

A breathtakingly cool portrayal of soldiering, a virtual inside
Perspective into today's premier land force, an entertaining

Ambush and wipe out for well-chosen high-potential madcaps,
Exploring its many gores and global opportunities, different

From other action games in this bloody genre, we emphasize
Verticality, teamwork, a square shaft and docility as means

Of achieving full-spectrum abjection, aggression and oblivion
To maximal pain, be it physical or mental, fugitive or eternal,

In oneself or another, whether man, woman, child or animal,
The torso zapped, snapped in half, hanging by a ligament,

The right leg swaying, the left shin crushed, blinded for life,
The clothing burnt off the front of a well-rendered anatomy.

Award-Winning Jejune Poetry, to be Encouraged

Always prompt to blast doors away, pass out kandies and kill,
The Asskickin' Armor-Plated Hummin' Boyz got da green light
For their next ripe picking, a backlit oasis complete with palms,
Scorpions, two-hump camels and derricks, but they ain't there
To chillax in no discounted Club Med, but to apply righteous,
Fearsome tactics, though the sun's nefarious glare, adrenalin
And narcotics make it hard to identify turbaned friends or foes.

Symmetries

Talking constant shoot, he forced the darn
Nude bleep bleep to smear loads on himself.
Later, when chased, he incontinently fled.

Scoring often, he refined his bitchin' techniques,
Flew freakin' home and stabbed her 76 times.

No fireworks, please, or he'll shoot in his dockers.

My Foreign Policy

As soon as the shooting started, I splurged
On a gorgeous, state of the art, plasma screen.
Before this war came on, there was nothing good
To watch on television, I couldn't focus, evenings
Were wasted on flops and penguins, but now,
My death wish slaked and placated by a fiesta
Of other people's corpses, my life's centered.

March 1, 2006

San Antonio, Texas—Since the USRA Track Management Group
took over San Antonio Speedway (SAS) last year, one of its main
goals has been the promotion of a family atmosphere at the
speedway. A frequent request from the fans and competitors was
the inclusion of children in the pit area. With the expansion of the
2006 schedule to include more nights of racing and the addition
of several touring shows, San Antonio Speedway has been
investigating the possibility of providing coverage to minors
through our insurance provider, Rand SE, Inc. SAS and Rand have
finally reached an agreement that will allow admission into the pit
area at any age. "We feel that this change would allow more
family involvement within the sport," said Rick Day, SAS General
Manager. "We invite everyone to come to San Antonio Speedway
this year and bring your families, whether you're sitting in the
grandstands or going into the pits. We're even looking forward to
someday seeing a driver's child become a crew chief. And since
these kids are probably helping with the work on the car during
the week, they'll now be closer to the action during the races."
Meanwhile, at the Brooke Army Medical Center, 26-year-old Sgt.
Joshua V. Youmans, 1st Battalion, 125th Infantry Regiment,
Michigan Army National Guard, finally passed away from injuries
sustained when a roadside bomb detonated near his Humvee
during combat operations in Habbaniya, Iraq on November 21,
2005. The very next day, however, March 2, 2006, veteran guard
Michael Finley, while still being paid millions of dollars by the
Dallas Mavericks, proved he was money for the San Antonio Spurs.
Finley scored 11 of his 15 points in the fourth quarter against his
former team, and the Spurs beat the Mavericks 98-89 in a

matchup of the top teams in the Western Conference. "It's always good to go against your friends, especially when you come out victorious," said Finley, who played nearly nine seasons in Dallas before being waived last summer under the NBA's one-time luxury tax amnesty provision. The Mavs still have to pay off his $52 million contract. With the victory, San Antonio leapfrogged Dallas into the top spot in the West. Both teams have 45-12 records, but the Spurs hold a 2-1 edge in head-to-head play. The win was also the 500th for San Antonio coach Gregg Popovich, who took over the team during the 1996-97 season. San Antonio led by four after three quarters, but extended that lead by shooting 11-for-19 in the fourth. Dallas got it down to 94-89 with 46 seconds to play when Dirk Nowitzki was fouled behind the 3-point line and made all three free throws. The Mavericks then started intentionally fouling the Spurs, who made most of them to maintain their lead. "I'm very disappointed with this loss," Dallas coach Avery Johnson said. "We realize who we were playing, but then again we gave them some easy baskets. We have just got to do a better job with our defense." Tony Parker led San Antonio with 23 points and Tim Duncan scored 15. Robert Horry, back after missing six games with an abdominal strain, made two 3-pointers and finished with 12. Jason Terry and Nowitzki each had 23 for the Mavs, who had won six straight. Josh Howard added 15. The 7-foot Nowitzki, defended most of the night by 6-foot-7 Bruce Bowen, shot only 6-for-15. "He can put pressure on you knowing that he's got two 7-footers right behind him," said Nowitzki, referring to Duncan and Nazr Mohammed. "Every time I tried to post him up, they came with a 7-footer to help on the baseline." Bowen said his strategy was to get a hand in Nowitzki's face and to bump him to keep him off-balance. "He's 7-feet, can shoot the 3 and can take you off the dribble, so he creates a lot of difficulties on the matchups," Bowen said. "A lot of bigs aren't quick enough to stay with him." Manu Ginobili made a runner off the opening tip, but the Mavericks ran off the next eight points and their defense did a good job denying close-in shots to the Spurs. Parker, one of the NBA's top inside scorers, started settling for jumpers after Nowitzki pinned his driving layup against the backboard early in the game. A jumper by Keith Van Horn extended the Dallas lead to 22-11 late in the first, but the Spurs cut it to 30-29 with about 4 minutes left in the half when an emboldened Parker squeezed a layup past Nowitzki's outstretched arm. The Mavs hit the next three baskets to make it 36-31 before Parker made a floater and then a fast-break layup to pull San Antonio within a point with 1:14 remaining. Dallas went up 46-40 early in the third on a follow by Nowitzki, but the Spurs took the lead with a 13-3 run capped by a breakaway dunk and a runner by Mohammed. Nowitzki, defended by Ginobili, put the Mavs back ahead with a three-point play and two free throws. San Antonio answered with a 3-pointer by Bowen and two foul shots by Parker to go up 68-64 after three quarters.

Instant Replays—Bolus or Eternal Returns?

162 bullshit happenings a year. First thing each morning,
I must check out the bullshit reckonings, even before I had
A chance to shoot, shower and shave. I can't start my day
Without knowing what happened last night, what went down.
I'm a team player, don't you understand? It's not about me.
If my bullshit logo won, then I'm vindicated—I'm half alive,
Sort of, for a minute or two, tops. If it lost, I'm nothing.

Dialectics

Each birth a disaster. A baby is always cute
Because of its huge, adult-size eyes, in spite of
Its small head. Its breath is clean, and not yet
Murderous. Each death occasions relief.

We're disarmed by its edible, poodle mass,
And its fumbling through the fun house maze
Of our wiggly, injurious tongue. Unlike immigrants,
It cannot retaliate with secret thoughts or words.

A child brings love, brightens the house. It's how
Life's supposed to be. On this cozy earth, earthquakes,
Tsunamis, droughts and plagues are always a godsend.
Once born, a rock wants to be a sated, successful rock.

Unitary Puff Paste

Living in Iowa, he scans the weather in Florida.
Living in Chicago, he checks, nearly every hour,
The Los Angeles traffic reports. Living in Italy,
He follows the Asociación del Fútbol Argentino.
Living in Buenos Aires, conversely, he watches
As many matches as possible of the Serie A.

It's important, you see, to know everything, because
Everything's bound together by an Intelligent Design
Of assisted suicide: bases, pipelines and the IMF.

Are You Refined?

I used to paint with linseed,
Now I paint with crude oil.

Draped in cheap oil and sweating oil,
Under an increasingly hot sun, I steer
An oil car, on oil, towards my oil job.

Look at that skyscraper made with oil!
Billboard-size minimalist oils decorating
Spanking lobbies of unctuous firms.

Before meals, I pray and take an oil pill.
To feel upper or downer, I chug a lug oil.

Massive Transitory Poetry

Purged of all human hang-ups,
I'm a friendly cognitive cog
In a cordial machine. In short,
I'm a competent bus driver.

O the various incidental, often erotic, contacts
Of living in a city: the stepping on heel collars,
The near-fatal car crashes, the skirted pats.

How do you translate my girlfriend's
White bits are missing into English?
[non sequitur, postmodern bit]

Don't say, I'm on the bus, declare
I'm in the bus, or, at the very least,
State, I'm with the bus. Capisce?

I grow crusty, ever crustier, shall I
Ride starboard, first or second deck,
Civil rights, larboard or shotgun?

Eroticism

United's stewardess' unusually wide brushes,
Intentionally, I think, against my iPod's tangle.

Holiday Inn's night owl clerk in Preoria,
A corn-syruped ex lacrosse wing, chirps,
"Just ring me if you need anything."

Consenting to loads of extra ketchup,
Burger King's pregnant teenager winks.

Investment Advices

Shimmering on the horizon, the four horsemen
Will arrive soon. Put all your liquid assets into
Baked beans, canned tuna and bandages.

After the almighty Dollar evaporates, the King's
English will shrivel. Therefore, toss your English
Dictionaries away, burn all of your English books.

Diminishing Addenda

Because of the chemical phthalate in plastic, dicks
Are shrinking—tell me all about it—sperm counts
Are way down, but not low enough, unfortunately,
To slow down this full-throttle-ahead fuck boat,
About to burn, capsize and sink. The seedy
Demilitarized zone between anus and dick,
Perinaion in Greek, is also contracting.

Banality

If you're lucky enough to grace this fragrant mud,
Even for a flash or two, don't give fucking a miss.

This fucking may be overrated, yeah, except to those
Who are curtailed from its lubricating access, yeah.

Free Jizz

Ebullient, habitual jailbirds
Can't help but pump, even
In icy solitary confinement.

To counter, the longest mensch
Must mesh as often as possible
With the lankiest women—Plato.

Thwarted by ribbed rubber,
Unfortunately, some mourn,
Masters of Arts and Science,
While genius gargoyles spout.

It's thundered that men and women of full age, without
Any hinderance due to passport, skin tone or religion,
Whether a punk, a poet, a lunatic or a preacher,
Have the right to marry and to found a family.

At the Goa rave, ballhogs, lollipops and witches
Circulating among doofs, tugboats and whales,
Multiply with calculators between their thighs.

Melodrama

This blade is sharp, thin, longest,
This blade doesn't stab but erases,
Like a schoolboy's eraser, it erases
Your face with my blood, or your blood,
All blood is the same, an amorous debt,

Incurred incrementally by pigs. Pigs
Know how to cry, who doesn't know?
Even flies sob each night.

All rivers fade into the ocean, a man blurs
Into his wife's shadow, if he's lucky, before
He rubs his eyes, then pulls out the knife.

Cruel and Singular Punishment

I have not raised my voice, I have not
Caused trouble, I have not stolen joints
Of meat, I have not spoken too much,
And yet [your name here] for the truth,
Wrongfully, and without reason, am I
Confined in this [your name here].

Add-On Spiels

Are you a woman who has never conceived,
Hates the idea of it, feeling sorry for yourself,
Despite cohabitation and exposure to a man's
Flawed or perfect wand, for at least two years?

Do you want to jelly your proud, miserable sperms,
To fertilize the lovely, laughing daughter, or perhaps
Granddaughter of the girl next door, several decades
After your gurgling joke of a life and farcical death?

Are your ankles fractured from a cursed, vanity spill?
Do you ingest beaucoup pills to remember or forget?

A Smooth Life

I have a smooth life and a bright future but I don't care
If I die soon because I'm too lazy to go on and maintain
All of my successes I've been in daycare since birth no one

Ever talks to me or changes my diaper I catch every disease
From everyone else but I also dish out my share I had sex
For the first time in kindergarten instead of protesting the war

Or whatever I watch porn all day what a douche bag I'm a lesbian
But I'm trying to turn myself straight for good I don't know why
There's nothing wrong with being gay I just hate women I like

Sleeping with them enough but I can't fathom spending the rest
Of my span with one of them scags they think they're so kawaii
It makes me sick each one latching on to a jalapeno beef jerky

In stone-washed jeans I hate straight porn but I've been inching
Towards straight sex by watching gay male porn at first I thought
It was disgusting but I've learnt to get off on it I obsess about

So many things from my horrible past things that happened
Before I was even born just kidding stupid errors I've made
Like a dumb comment I'd obsess about for weeks on end I may

Have an as-yet-unidentified mental illness I can't for the life of me
Stop thinking of the word snatch attack whenever I see a knife
Or anything sharp I just want to stab myself or any nearby flesh

I dread the day I'll have to do this because I'll certainly do it soon
Whenever I cross a bridge I just want to drive right off I'd ask myself
So many weird questions such as why are women's buttons on the left?

Why doesn't anyone help me? God damn it how come I never score
With a good looking one?! I just love to look at breasts although
I'm neither a man nor a lesbian I must own the world record

For most masturbations in a day a week or a lifetime I masturbate
First thing in the morning last thing at night of course I masturbate
In my sleep I prefer masturbation to actual sex I'd rather masturbate

Than fuck Reese Weatherspoon after all who could possibly know you
And love you better than yourself? Soon I'll have a heart attack and die
While whacking off I guess I just don't dig it when people bring me

To a climax something about another person getting me to that point
Makes me feel weak and exploited sex is not pointless it's fun as hell
And enjoyable it's just the end that sucks I just can't do intercourse

Right now I need a decade at least to work on myself physically
Mentally and spiritually before I can have the confidence to let
Someone fall in love with me again if you just keep yakking people

Will ignore everything you say even the most horrible or vicious
Or incriminating once I couldn't help but yank it out and spray it
At her left eye or maybe it was her right eye with a straight face

I said to him it was an OK size but I was laughing deeply inside
I felt so embarrassed for him sometimes I stretch my nutsack
Over a flashlight I get so ridiculously horny I just want to shove

The entire Milky Way up up inside of me last week I went down
On my best friend it was pretty hilarious and enjoyable but I still love
The cock sometimes I fantasize about screwing dead people young

Pretty girls of course with all of their cutesy limbs and organs intact
There's nothing more beautiful than innocence especially expired
Innocence once as I was making love to my lover I accidentally

Blurted out I love you I feel so humiliated I think I'll leave her soon
During sex I always wear a headphone to groove to my favorite band
I'm addicted to go-go bars I prefer lap dances from total strangers

To intercourse with my lovely wife I'd fantasize about giant breasts
And penises hovering in the sky like Chinese kites when I'm with her
It's like the 4th grade all over again the name calling teasing playful

Grabbing whispering secrets awkward silences long gazes shoving
Kicking feeling warm heart beating faster I'm a method actor
Who's intrigued by suicide though I doubt I would ever make

That final cut I can only make love to one song and one song only
Is it wrong to obsess about doorknobs? Of course we know
That all you want is to fuck us fine all we want is something good

Looking to make our friends envious when we're out a hard fuck
And a fat wallet everyday I turn on the news hoping something bad
Has happened in America instead of donating to the third world

I buy shoes my husband reads all the time my complexity tells me
I'm not an animal I'm not proud really of my contradictions should I
Feel unattractive because my boyfriend's prick is rather small

And can't stay up for very long at all?

Pixel Jerks

You totally control the dancer, you decide
How she dances, what she wears, even
Her expressions, the music she moves to,
Have her writhe or spin just when and how,
Make her laugh, sneer, wink or slap herself.

DYNAMIC HAIR COLORS
DYNAMIC OIL HER UP
DYNAMIC SPOTLIGHT COLORS
DYNAMIC AMBIENT LIGHTS
DYNAMIC LIPSTICK COLORS
DYNAMIC TATTOOS

Unbelievably realistic models
Tight details where it counts
Total Control Mode

COOL COWGIRL OUTFIT
CHEERLEADER OUTFIT
WICKED DEVIL GIRL
NUN OR G.I. JANE
SWEATY HOYDEN
SPANKING MAID
JUNGLE GIRL

Shake those!
Work that pole!
Show us that!
Blow us a kiss!
All natural! Nice.
You're in control.

Jiggle, tongue, rock out, kiss me.
Ice Cream, Whip Cream, Banana.
I love you. Hi! What's your name?
Bend over, sleep with me tonight.
What's your phone number?

As she dances, watch her expressions fluctuate,
Shift your mouse to catch her from all angles,
Before you strip away her excess pixels.

Raw, Windswept Capital, Regulated

To legally work nude, you must be employed
By someone who possesses a nude permit.

Nude means being devoid of an opaque covering
Over the genitals, pubic hair, buttocks, perineum,
Anus or anal region of a person, or any portion
Of the female breast at or below the areola, or
Male genitals in a clearly turgid state, even
If completely and opaquely covered. Nude,

You shall not be within six feet of a patron.
You shall not intentionally touch him or her,
Or allow a patron to intentionally touch you,

Whether nude or not. Nude, you must not work
Between 2 and 6 AM. You shall not encourage
Or allow the fondling or even casual brushing
Of your genitals, pubic region, buttocks, anus
Or breasts, sex acts, normal or perverted,
Actual or simulated, including intercourse,
Oral copulation, or sodomy, masturbation,
Actual or simulated, or excretory functions.

Concave Serial Loop

Below the belt? Whose belt? I have a lot
Of sick sex to sort out, yes, and no, this
Is not a confessional gaud. The bat buffs
The lathered beaver, the bored chicken screws
The lewd duck, and I would certainly applaud
A tactical nuke on my mother-in-law, so help me,
God. Amen.

A Few Days, Paid by the Night

Just got back from there. Only drunks
Yoyoing up and down, yakking, giggling
All night long. Couldn't gain oblivion at all
On a bobbing mattress.

As misfortunes rushed to their eyeballs and foreheads,
They vomited, cursed, but kept on singing. On the walls,
A thousand spider husks wavered. I swear

I saw something like a melancholic gecko, longing
For an abstract illusion, an improbable color or a trite,
Romantic smell. He writhed like half of my soul, at least.

The damp spot on the ceiling kept on weeping, a pubescent girl
With fresh lipstick, having just chucked her egg for the first time,
Her hair not yet dyed a breezy color.

Behind the moldy curtain, a moldy anatomy. Never lit,
The new lightbulb had already become obsolete. Leaving,
I crossed a happening mess, lumpy with creations. Let's

Meet in the next life, right here, OK?

Generosity

A penny from God, a discount one, my dick is sacred
And not to be liberally displayed, au gratis, to the hoi polloi.
No one has seen it, not even my wife of seven decades.
Maybe I've dreamt it,

But there's a nagging memory of my mama milking it
Against my stiff will. Annealed is the right word. Soon
As I close my eyes, I can see her multi-ringed fingers
In snappy resolution. Then later,

Much later, a pastel colored woman beckoned,
"Here, come here." It was midnight and she was sobbing
Because she had never seen my dick.

Geopolitical

Grungy anarchists, survivalists,
They crap on Bismarck in Berlin,
Queen Victoria in Edinburgh,
Abstract sculptures and scores
Of nobodies, trying to munch from
Brown paper bags. They lay siege
To each square on earth, except those
Of Ho Chi Minh City, my hometown.

Birds hate loud noises. Bombs
Scared them away? Hell no,
We ate them all.

Prelude

Please don't shoot me, I only have a dollar
A day, plastic flip-flops and a hovel. Please
Don't stab me, I have no cash, only credit
Cards, a BMW, a yacht and a McMansion.
Please don't bomb me, I had everything
Already, before you came.

Refrain

Well, then, if an alien object, something tiny
Even, like a grain of bullshit, is persistently
Lodged within the brain, there's nothing to do
But to shoot the motherfucker. My eyes
Are alien to me, their defects hindering
My already dire discourse with the real,
This lake here, them privates. That's why
I must shoot the motherfuckers.

Aesthetic Probity

Man ripped own ears off, disgusted by a pusillanimous note.
Man ripped own nose off, offended by a glancing equivocal odor.
Man ripped own eyes out, outraged by an extraneous
Exclamation point!

Later, he ate a futile, pointless and hapless sandwich,
An absolutely no-go-zone sandwich,
A ridiculous, degrading and criminal sandwich. Retching,
He ripped his own mouth from his face.

Flexing Man Reflecting

With a boing of luck and a lot of hard work,
Money and cheating, I can become the world
Deluded champion, at last, infantile division.
Thank you, Jesus. Shit, or get off the pot.

My siege mentality gives me
An unfair advantage, you say?
My continent-size ego, my corn syrup?
My spiritual suction, whatever that is?

Quantifiable virtues are all that matter,
Speeding, earning, killing, kicking ass.
Artistic scores are oxymorons.

This sport should be banned in every goddam country
In the free, semi-free and unfree world, but my own.

Whazzit to you, pisswad?

Torino 2006

Yes, it's true they wheeled out a laminated blow-up
Of Boccioni's "Unique Form of Continuity in Space,"
Rechristianed "Futuristic Man" by the media. Hundreds
Of Italians doing Tae Kwon Do punches and kicks, evoking
The Seoul Olympics of 1988, then a red Ferrari, a symbol
Of speed, machismo, ingenuity and waste, stole the show,
Screeching and spun as fireworks rocketed and exploded.
Yoko then appeared in shades, to earnestly encourage us
To pray for peace, on the eve of wars over waste and speed.
The original futuristic man, Marinetti, once declared that war
Is a form of universal hygiene. Imagine.

Rock Legends

I lika Lennon John. I lika
Very much The Rolling Stans.

Rocks are cool. About 15,000 years ago,
A sandstone no larger than a Bible rolled
From present-day Spilby, Lincolnshire
To present-day Blaxhall, Suffolk, described
By Ewart Evans as "an out-of-the way village,
Neglected and to a certain extent despised,
With little claim to any distinction at all."

Ploughed up from the queachy soil in the 1800's,
This rock has grown steadily to its current weight
Of at least 5 tons.

At this rate, estimate physicists, it will equal
The mass of the earth in 3,000 years, that is,
There will be another earth atop this one
In 3,000 years.

Nature Freaks

Sometimes I forget that this world came
From fresh herring, that these people come
From solid herring stock. Lovely Bianca Black

Will soon be wedded to one Chien Meow, I see
Very clearly now how herring has brought us all
Together, under the lych gate, waiting, as always,

For the damn priest to tuck away his sin, before
He lowers us, one by one, into the bog, minus
Our blameless nuts and titties.

Affixions

Here the young like to skate about
In their gauzy glaze, while the old
Don crusty mud as they mosey.

Horse hair extension or tall turban crowns
An upended jockey, who's checking out
All them fine, slurry chicks in stilettos.

(In this 1 billion-horse boonies, all the men
Are 5 foot 3 or less, and shrinking fast.)

Over the crotch, an embroidered arch,
Or just air, when the temperature's right.

Tell all the gangly fucks to shun vertical stripes.
As for the squat screws—no horizontal.

Let's Think This Over

Only thing worse than dying once,
No doubt, is to get struck twice
By the mother of all muggers.
Once by bullet, once by ale;
Once by falling, once crushed.
On the other hand, you'll get
Two funerals and two graves,
Side by side, perhaps. Here lies
Your name, who departed this life
On such an illegible date. And here lies
Your name, again, who split this life
On another illegible date. No more
Naked pigs feeding in a field for you,
No more cows merging in the mist.

Deadly Bravado

Itchythology: a probe and survey into
The myriad causes of itching. Let's talk
About death instead. Dying is certainly
Not an au courant thing to do. Let's hope
It is forthright, linear and not an endlessly
Tedious workshop. Before you stride over

My bone mess, over and over, I'd like to X
Another mega contract, worthy of my still
Erect stature.

*

Death ambushes us
From below. Lusting
To know what drawn
And quartered feels like,
He fondles his thanatos
Without blinking once.

*

Meanwhile, the sappy and sappily vanquished
Are dripping in frustration. Distilled to shades,
They hump and are humped by shades.

*

Already humped, in papyrus, you wait
Across a dim, slushy street. It snows,
But not nearly cold enough to stick.

Optical Axes

The trees sway, that's nothing, the world itself
Vibrates. A black curtain drops from the sky.
All the erased scenes reappear, tactile, true,
The beckoning, accusing faces. Promiscuous,
They cancel each other out. "Do I know you?"
"Do you remember me?" "Of course, I do."
Have I seen so much? I haven't lived a day.

Poltroon Zen near Mallaig

Bonked from this bobbing limbo, I want to encore
As a fluffy one with a black face, not a horny ram
But an ordinary sheep scramming from the toots,
Clanks and puffs of a belaboring train, otherwise,
I'll keep my head down 24/7, stuffing my haggis.

Bairn in Bothy on Hogmanay Demanding Cadeaux

How do you signature discomfort, pain or displeasure?
If you abject something, like, really undressed, a necessity,
How do you ping ping about getting it? Do you feel flushed?
Have you ever effaced a whorl? Alive? That's OK. Do you
Typecast your eyes with your mouth or hands? Do you
Typecast other people's present with your own past?
What time is it? Are you dozed by large numbers?
Thrilled, even, by record breaking numbers? Are you in-
Fatuated with the zigzags and hues of your own clothes?
Differently, are you just schnooking around or cloacal?

English as a Fifth Language

A very bad fan faces
A cool wall, just like random intimacy
After mouth washing. Make love happen

Sometimes. Remember, wherever

You go, a body of water is often brown,
Green, silver or black, but rarely blue.

I'll never sit at the board, she kvetched,
I've the wrong chair [too many wheels].

A broken fan faces
An icy wall. In Brixton,
I saw a fey cow atop
A wind chime, and a man
Living inside his guitar.

Was it electric?

The eel ate his cord.
The man ate his eel.

Guide to London

London (pronounced Lun Lun) is a glorious, grim city by the Damn
River. Known for its chicken tikka masala, London was founded by
Romans in 43 A.D. It has been destroyed several times: in 61 by
the Icenic Queen, Boudicca—see sexy statue across from Big Ben;
in 1666 by a great fire; during World War II by German
bombers, and in the 1980's by Margaret Thatcher, the Milk
Snatcher. A vast subway system, the Tube, connects Londoners to
every corner of the world. One only has to groove down an
escalator at Piccadilly Circus to emerge dazed, minutes later, in
Camden (New Jersey), Hong Kong, Beirut or Kingston, Jamaica.
Famous Londoners, past and present, include Karl Marx, George
Orwell, Bloody Mary, Simone Weil, David Blaine, the Hunchback
of Notre Dame (disputed) and the One-Eyed Sheik. Whatever you
do, don't eat at Mr. Wu's Buffet on Wardour Street. For £5, all
you get is fuckin' onion. It sucks.

The Sailors' Reading Room

When in Southwold, a lovely village on the coast of Suffolk, it is imperative that one visits the Sailors' Reading Room. The widow of sea captain Charles Rayley had it built in 1863 to provide fishermen, sea dogs, mariners and buccaneers with a sane, non-alcoholic haven to socialize, and yes, to chew over an occasional paragraph from a large-print book, a pamphlet, or glance at the headlines of a newspaper: Teen Killed For Kicks, Laughed At Trial; Plonker In Stuke, Stuck Head In Microwave. When I dropped by the Sailors' Reading Room on January 20th, 2006, I saw five busty figureheads, colorful, tilting, condescend from the back wall, vitrines filled with models of beach yawls, longshore punts, schooners, battle class destroyers, but no sailors. Behind a lit door—Game Room Members Only—one could hear stout, rattling sabres, windswept, clattering dentures or, no less improbable, just a game of scrabble.

A Decayed Fishermen's Hospital

This Hospital was Erected at the expense of the Corporation of Great Yarmouth, Anno Domini 1702. At a Common Council on the 3rd of 1711, it was ordered that no person be admitted under the age of 60. That only Fishermen be admitted. By this we mean someone who has spent the Better, more hopeful part of his Life in Trapping or Ensnaring Fish, including, Literally & Figuratively, most cold-blooded aquatic vertebrate having Scales & Breathing through Gills, all varieties of Shellfish, such as Shrimps, Lobsters, Oysters, Clams, Scallops, Crayfish, Crabs and Winkles, as well as the Rare Mammal who has somehow managed to make a Passable Life of it in the Storm-Tossed Sea. The Terrestrial Snail cannot enter into this equation. If a Fisherman is married, his Wife shall escort him until Death, but should Any become a Widower while in Hospital, he must not assume another Sacred bond without Sanction of the Committee. Should he Die, Suddenly or not so Suddenly, and leave behind a relieved or Distraught Widow, his Bereaved will be asked very Delicately to abandon this Premise within two Weeks. She is neither Fisherman nor Fisherwoman, after all, and This is clearly Designated as a Fisherman's Hospital. The aforementioned Deceased shall be Perfunctorily yet Ceremoniously Released into the sea, in Ash form if Desired, since his Spiritual Home & Origin is no more than a Vigorous stone's throw from this Lovely Ground. Lastly, please be advised that the Outward Gate is locked at exactly 9 of the clock every night, although, Frankly, the wickedly Spiked yet rather Low Fence poses no insurmountable obstacle for any Drunk-Yet-Still-Nimble excluded Fisherman.

Sandettie

Skipper mistakes Calais for Kent.
Dover lifeboat had to be sent out
To rescue a lost yachtsman who
Thought he was near Ramsgate
When he was 10 miles off Calais, in France.

The skipper of Marie Louise
Contacted Dover Coastguard
On Saturday night. He had sailed
From Southwold, Suffolk and thought
He was near Ramsgate but the port control
Could not find him. He was told to sail to a buoy,
Then report back what it said, which turned out to be Sandettie.
The lifeboat crew found the yacht's compass was faulty. "The skipper
Of this vessel was crossing some of the busiest shipping lanes
In the world without, it would appear, much navigational
Knowledge or experience," said Dover Coastguard
Watch manager Gary Brown. The coastguard
Decided sending a lifeboat was the safest
Way to get the moron back home.

Spiralling Jetty

They often confuse ships with the whale that saved them
During many close calls. They think everything's a ship.
They name their children after sunken ships. They often
Call their mom "Titanica." In the evening, they stand alone
In their landlocked rooms, looking at the brown, mossy
Bricks across an alley, and hear, they swear, a foghorn
Calling them home, when they're already fuckin' home.

Bloody Cruise

Standard of work is passable and the accommodation faux luxurious.
Nevertheless, things creak often and certain squalor issues, inevitably,
From you know where and where. I saved my life for this, only to have it
Befouled by sebaceous crooks and joke compensations, adding spat insults
To turf and surf sickness. No scum on draft, should we mutiny, disembark
Or sail on?

Poetical Pedagogics

Many Western poets gain niggardly fame
By surfing the sonnet, while those of the East
Often avail themselves of the economical haiku.
Images are organically the fun foci of poetry.
Paired with inapt similes, they can provide slits
For uncivil poets to startle.

Phoneme Nugget

Rotate this phoneme, study it,
Then examine its base closely.
See that hairline crack? Sniff it,
Son. I'm not a butcher, but I know
What I like.

What Words Do

They cannibalize each other. The weakest ones
Are merely parasites. Grafting words onto words,
The wishy-washy don't trim away what's superfluous,
Resulting in ghastly weed gardens. Words, especially
Wrong and pointless ones, like to flit about, like bugs.

Tyranny and Succor

Hogging the biosphere, he chatters
Only to deny everyone else's existence.
The tongue is a persistent wand. When
A mouth cannot shut up, it should
Have something nice stuffed in it.

They're always blathering about themselves, of course.
She's waxing about her nice, petite ears. He's spinning
About his oddly shaped nose. Freedom of expressions
Must be balanced against freedom against speech.

Nothing is true, sure enough, unless in print.
No one dies privately, alone. Dead, he waits
Three days to read about it in the newspaper.

Wrong

Foreigners always talk too loud in public. That's because
Most of them are deaf. A man could be spilling his innards
About his deformed children, his home burning, his tortured
Curriculum vitae, but none of it makes sense, because he
Has, at best, a jury-rigged, tinfoil grasp of your grammar.

Cheapies?

Though ant-size and often meaningless, words
Are still commodities, to be bartered and sold.
Gaia, carnage, fucking, your future and forests
Are constantly converted into frazzled phrases
Wrapped in bright, childish colors, then peddled
At the stressed entrances of subway stations.

Dissatisfied with the transubstantiation of wet skin
Into dry, flaky words, he subscribes to a cool web
Pictorial advertising naked hunting and gathering
Amateurs, frolicking in mud, for $29.99 a month.

Man Wearing Glasses

Plucked from the land, I must be taught
How to cross the street to order a steak.

Removed from the soil, I inject
Dirt into every article of speech.

I cannot look at any landscape, a lake,
A canyon, a cave or a volcano, without
Recalling some presumptuous painting.

Sap green smudges flecked with scarlet lake.
Naples yellow dabs abutting umber webbing.
Above, a wash of indigo-tinted cremitz white.

I can't even tell a male from a female mallard.

Painting Challenges

Forget majestic sunset, homestead or discreet nudity,
Paint something so (genuinely or fraudulently) salving,
The viewer will never feel forsaken again, no matter
How horrible his life may turn out, whether
From an exotic or common affliction.

Forget the twelve keys to great compositions,
Paint something so horrifying, it'll ruin the structural
And surface integrity of a man's physiognomy,
And desolate his soul permanently.

HF ICBW BFN

End of day,
Face to face,
Fine by me.

On the other hand,
Over and out,
Just a sec,
I rest my case,
Unpleasant visual,
That stinks!

Girlfriend, boyfriend, best friend,
Never mind, one of these days,
I love you, see you later,
I'm not a lawyer.

Way to go, you'll be sorry,
Sorry, I could not resist,
Get a life, take your time,
Same place same time,
Sick of me yet? Speak.

So stupid it's not funny,
To be honest, take care,
Between me and you,
Same stuff, different day,
What's up? Thanks a lot.

FORTUNES

fortune n° 841
February 12, 2007

Read about "transparent white" in the afternoon, dream of Bianca
Blanco at night, slide into third base, headfirst, of course,
entangling my goatee. How fortunate I don't babble during sleep,
dependable wife still snoring beside me. Abrupt knife fantasy
discounted as spilled subconscious.

Filed under: destiny   Comments (0)

fortune n° 507
February 1, 2007

The spanking new shower door slides open, leaving just enough
space for a fat man to sidle, startling a war-torn, deluded planet.
How fortunate my stem isn't more unwieldy. A stuck exit averted.

Filed under: destiny   Comments (0)

fortune n° 506
January 18, 2007

For decades I observed myself from the side and back, even in
complete darkness, entwined with another, sympathetic or just
drunk unfortunate. I couldn't jar my grammar lose after three
minutes, even, forgetting often to suck the other side. Danke gosh
for cheap beer, which could add another two or three minutes.

Filed under: destiny   Comments (0)

fortune n° 485
January 16, 2007

Bobby Byrd tells me that ni modo is Spanish for oh well, at least
along the border between us, us and more of us, where the good,
the evil and simply wide eyed brush legs under a tacky electric
blanket. How fortunate. Ni modo, oh well, ni modo es el motto de
mi vida.

Filed under: destiny   Comments (0)

fortune n° 421

January 14, 2007

A German speaking Jew in a new Czech nation dreamt up a small menagerie of talking and hybrid animals, from an "odradek" to chatty jackals and a celebrity ape who first learnt to spit, then, in a moment of triumph, blurted out, "Hello!" Long circular walks and smudgy dreams of Palestine. Seeing no place, no future for himself, he could never procreate. Like me and you and you. How fortunate. Let's fuck!

Filed under: destiny   Comments (0)

fortune n° 265

December 29, 2006

My wife and I have a great sense of humor. Each time we have sex, she said, I wish I were a lesbian. I just bought you a strapped-on dildo, I said, so you could fuck me up the ass.

Filed under: destiny   Comments (0)

fortune n° 221
December 26, 2006

Sitting in the food court at a shopping mall, eating a corporate Chalupa Supreme, besieged and comforted by my similars, in smells and everything, I overheard, "There is this girl, there always is." Then, from a diverse end, "I could pretend to love a self-defecating, drooling retard if he paid me enough." Self-defecation, I often hear, is only a clumsy, messy disguise for self-love. Ni modo, you're not that stupid or ugly, etc.

Filed under: destiny   Comments (0)

fortune n° 218
December 24, 2006

Like everybody else, I prefer a screen. Outside, strange leaves, commerce and explosions. Though nearly blind, I must caress, sigh and lick this or that picture box, lit from inside.

Filed under: destiny   Comments (0)

fortune n° 210
December 20, 2006

To have another tongue inside one's mouth, to lend one's tongue to
another, to swallow ten tongues at once, to stick one's seasoned or
virgin tongue into unlikely panoramas. Pity the proud, fearful
tongue cowering inside its cold safe, watching the same old same
old.

Filed under: destiny   Comments (0)

fortune n° 192
December 18, 2006

With one foot in North Korea, one in South, I write a poem. With
my heart in Mexico, liver in the USA, I write a poem. With the tip
of my nose in Great Yarmouth, Ajaccio, Dien Bien Phu, I nudge and
smear borders.

Filed under: destiny   Comments (0)

fortune n° 166
December 13, 2006

To be scribbled on a postcard: in the USA, even the houses are
homeless, pointing elsewhere, yearning to get out. This warehouse,
with its fake beams, to England; that "hacienda," with its jive
adobe, to Mexico. Many swear by another galaxy.

Filed under: destiny   Comments (0)

fortune n° 137
December 5, 2006

Some guy named Salmon says, "My mother-in-law, before she was my mother-in-law"—just hearing that word twice pains me— "I had to win her over, so as to win over her daughter, you know, so I decided to stroke her up really good, in all the right places, you know, comfort the old girl a little, froth her up some, and she wasn't even that old, to tell you the truth."

Filed under: destiny   Comments (0)

fortune n° 136
December 1, 2006

Come on now, multiply your fear by a thousand, your greed by a thousand, your kung fu reflex by a thousand, because we're going to eat each other for breakfast, lunch and tapas, naked under a white sun, our artsy fig leaves already burnt for heat.

Filed under: destiny   Comments (0)

fortune n° 130
November 28, 2006

"Best hell," my stoic, white-haired, downer of a father advised. "You must best hell."

Filed under: destiny   Comments (0)

fortune n° 128
November 26, 2006

I open a rare book: "Before mankind discovered calcium, people existed without bones. Equally pliant and desirable, sinuous men and women slither on the ground, greeting each other with their tongues only, since they had no flapping jaws to make sounds, nor teeth to flash their benignity. Esoteric words like skeletal, bony or boner were used only in the worst poetry."

Filed under: destiny   Comments (0)

David Larsen sent me his translation-in-progress of Ibn Khalawayh's compilation of the 400 plus names of the lion, "The Oceanic," "One Who Equals Ten," "Bad Fortune," "The Unwelcome Sight," "Huge and Lengthy," "Whose Food Has Bones In It"… Ibn Khalawayh also listed 200 names and epithets for the snake. Today, our lions, snakes and tigers have become cartoons. In 2001, I saw a wooden something at a dusty, cobwebbed temple in Saigon. Worshippers had left grains of uncooked rice on its head and rubbed fat into its mouths. He was in the shape and size of a dog, with only a coat of yellow paint and black stripes to persuade me otherwise. Only a century ago, the Vietnamese would have called him "Mr. Tiger." A tiger's claw was worn as a talisman to ward off tiger attacks. After killing Mr. Tiger, the hunter's first order of business was to burn off his whiskers, believed to be poisonous.

Filed under: destiny   Comments (0)

fortune n° 99
November 20, 2006

It's already too late in the day to make certain crucial, cosmetic adjustments. My head never found your armpit, unfortunately, although I was willing, eager even, to zigzag in deep pain, figuratively speaking. A dislocated mindset, nine broken thoughts, smeared with a splayed brush on the cheapest paper. Even before the next outbreak of irregular warfare, catastrophic or needling, disruptive attacks, our empty shelves stretch into a non-haloed eternity.

Filed under: destiny   Comments (0)

fortune n° 93
October 30, 2006

Untouched fingers like weisswurscht twirling long red hair, train and mind rocking, the dance, the scream, her teenaged tympanums preoccupied. Cut it open, then suck, or leave the lower part intact, fuss out the good stuff with a fork.

Filed under: destiny   Comments (0)

fortune n° 88
October 28, 2006

Frowning, he kept baying, "For those who don't know," during his 90-minute blah blah blah performance, culminating with, "Do you understand?" Dribbling words is a compulsion shared by idiots and geniuses alike, a survival tactic by those already sloshing in slogans, life-sapping sentences and wrinkled, washed-out wisdom. This rubbery aperture moves this way and that, a natural opening without meat or mint, still fragrant, too clever, according to some, that sucking sound.

Filed under: destiny   Comments (0)

fortune n° 71
October 24, 2006

Towards the end of their disjointed, not-too-funny dialogue, she flung this banality at his nonstick noggin, "Bon mot, syllogistic ping pong rallies are slope-shouldered substitutions for anxiety-ridden, atavistic whoopees." "You got it backward," he countered, mumbling. Nothing had been or would ever be accomplished. Should he apologize to each woman, but one? She accuse each man, but one?

Filed under: destiny   Comments (0)

fortune n° 49
October 20, 2006

The colors are clean, antiseptic, alpine, Innsbruck as seen from a slow-moving train, Heidi's face during sleep, minty, but the configuration is funky, nasty, disturbingly organic, yet another inappropriate eruption of sexual panic, resulting in fondly remembered, unspeakable seepages and songs.

Filed under: destiny   Comments (0)

fortune n° 45
October 16, 2006

Considering the heft, aroma and bouncing nature of it all, he reflects that there are basically two types, those who need to be envied, the braggarts who smear mud on everyone, and those who crave pity. I am so in debt, never a decent, melodic sequence of oral sex, clogged up, no time, with so many lush, crappy poems to be unleashed.

Filed under: destiny   Comments (0)

fortune n° 44
September 28, 2006

I eat much marvelous beef, yes, eyeballs of beef, tongues, cheat
of beef, like mathematically perfect buns, my mouth yearns to
devour every other mouth, as smart as cows, cheese in our moldy
mouths, already old, because we live in same-same caves, like, on
television.

Filed under: destiny   Comments (0)

fortune n° 30
September 24, 2006

The black kettle is a burning cat, evoking impatient concern. The
toilet has a lovely, latinate name, and some moons ago was lusted
over by sad, diminutive men, sighing in the dark. The couch is a
cheerful dump. The bed creaks, but rarely, if ever and ever and
ever.

Filed under: destiny   Comments (0)

He's not dead, he's digested. Unperturbed. Haven't you noticed
how these fuckin' foreigners always get the "foot" and "feet"
wrong? As in, "What happens when a twelve-feet python swallows
a sixteen-feet alligator?"

Filed under: destiny   Comments (0)

Before committing suicide by a small firearm, he decided to check his email one last time, and received these spams:

"And postlude in resignation," from Haley Conner
"But sanguineous or sault," from Tania Walking
"To is vote," from Marian Fritz.

There is also an invitation to become friends with Genesis Freak (female), 17 years old:

Subject: hi.. how's it going?

Body: So, i guess the time has arrived for me to start using this account. I can hold back no more! I took a gander though your page and well, I liked what I saw.. :p

So, i think me and you should be friends, because you seem pretty fun, and maybe even cute! (it's everso hard to tell in this digital world :)

Filed under: destiny   Comments (0)

fortune n° 1
September 14, 2006

I begin my novel, at last: Tonight the wind stinks, the clouds sag, as
usual, my hands scoured white, no money, my face and moon a
velvety black. The rain strips us of our discounted pretensions,
restoring a violent innocence to our much crumpled, disused eros.

Filed under: destiny   Comments (0)

POETRY BRIEFS

Fleeting Feathers: the Complete Poems of Humphrey McCaw
475 pages. Pelican Grove Press. $21.95

Humphrey McCaw is perhaps our greatest avian poet. No winged
creature was too repulsive or lightweight to escape his dartingly
sharp eye. He penned thousands of rhymes and near rhymes
about jackdaws, grackles, blue tits, red tits, bearded tits, the
annoying red grouse, the red-necked grebe, great bustards, wax
wings, wheatears, night jars, winchats, sand martins, hoopoes, wry
necks, blue throats and blue jays... Wry and persistent, he
repeatedly probed the myriad complicated implications of the
common magpie, as in this eponymous near classic:

> Half black, half white, multicultural
> Before its time? Not quite, the moor hen
> Is even red, brown and yellow.

Often branded a realist, even a photo-realist, McCaw was not
above caprice or goofy anachronism:

> Dutch treat—a dodo took flight
> Among the ho's of Amsterdam.
> In the middle of my life, between
> The Oude-Zijds-Voorburgwal &
> The Oude-Zijds-Achterburgwal,
> I heard my kettle boil.

Sometimes, he even went dada:

ooh eh EH ooh eh EEK ooh ehhh

ooh eh EEK EEK ooh ehh – vee vee

ooh eh EEE – EHHHHHHH

["14th Way of Looking at a Blackbird"]

Born in 1936 on the remote Scottish island of St. Kilda, McCaw made the near fatal mistake of migrating to Freemont, California in 1969, where he remained for the rest of his life, working in the microchip industry, yet all was not lost, obviously. Deprived of his beaked, gizzarded, feathered and occasionally-tarred friends, McCaw compensated himself—and us, habitues of English—with an exquisite, unmatched syntactical aviary. Aloof and sheepish— some say mousy—McCaw never hung out with other Bay Area poets, and even claimed to have never visited San Francisco. He refused to give readings or lectures, and when San Jose State University baited him with a tenure-track position in 1983, he turned down its relatively small class load and not-too-insulting salary. McCaw simply had no patience for anything that would distract from his fierce focus on birds. He loved them for what they were. In a rare interview, McCaw insisted that birds were not stand-ins for humans in his copious oeuvre: "Birds are only birds, but humans can be anything, even birds." A circular logician, perhaps, but a very fine poet indeed.

Selected Translations
Reggis Tongue
899 pages. Noioso. $29.95.

The sudden appearance of Reggis Tongue must qualify as one of the biggest literary stories of 2006. (Generally, one should never use the word "sudden," because, frankly, nothing is ever sudden. Suddenly they divorced, the world will suddenly end! No, son, it's been ending for a while.) With 12 volumes of translations published in frantic succession, Reggis Tongue suddenly staked his claim as the greatest translator, perhaps, of our time. Granted, there is nothing sexy about translating poems. When triumphant, one becomes merely invisible, but with the smallest blip, lapse or blunder, then abrupt universal ridicule, infamy, then gradual oblivion. For those who've been dozing for the last 12 moons, let me adumbrate essentially the aforementioned volumes, in order of publication:

1. The Complete Guilluame Apollinaire, translated by Reggis Tongue (Stochastic Shack 2006).
2. The Complete Antonin Artaud, translated by Reggis Tongue (Fawcett, Strauss & Giroux 2006).
3. The complete Cesar Vallejo, translated by Reggis Tongue (Xenograft Editions 2006).
4. The Complete Vicente Huidobro, translated by Reggis Tongue (Blue Decimal 2006).
5. The Complete Ingeborg Bachman, translated by Reggis Tongue (University of Baja California Press 2006).
6. The Complete Paul Celan, translated by Reggis Tongue (Community College of Northern Virginia Press 2006).

7. The Complete Amelia Rosselli, translated by Reggis Tongue (Hash House Press 2006).
8. The Complete Wislawa Szymborska, translated by Reggis Tongue (Vantage 2006).
9. The Complete Miroslav Holub, translated by Reggis Tongue (Vallecula Press 2006)
10. The Complete Attila Josef, translated by Reggis Tongue (Colon Press 2006).
11. The Complete Nina Cassian, translated by Reggis Tongue (Semi-Colon Press 2006).
12. The Complete Nazim Hikmet, translated by Reggis Tongue (Cecum Press 2006).

Correct me if I'm wrong, but that's 12 major poets, some of them quite difficult, if not impossible, converted from 9 mutually-hostile languages. No single mind should contain so much incongruity. Clayton Eshleman, Pierre Joris, Michael Hamburger, Eliot Weinberger and the rest of them should feel nothing but shame and disappear promptly from the face of this earth! But it's not just volume, girth and length that distinguish Reggis Tongue, it's his modus operandi. In the preface to his just-released "Selected Translations," Tongue stated unabashedly: "Slovenly translators— bums, basically—think they have to choose between music and sense. To pin down meanings, many of them squash the tune. To ape the melody, they ditch or deface the semaphores. They don't realize that syntax is melody. A translator must ignore the indigenous drumming echoing in his lumpy head and obey the alien word-order, rhythm of what's he's translating. Make it strange—never try to domesticate a foreign poem! As for meanings, what's keeping a translator, experienced or novice, from buying an electronic dictionary?" Sounds good, sort of, but how does it work in practice? Let's look at Tongue's rendition of Apollinaire's "Le Pont Mirabeau," a much-beloved poem that's been assassinated repeatedly over the years by everyone from Richard Wilbur to Donald Revell, to the Pogues. Here are the first six lines of the original:

> Sous le pont Mirabeau coule la Seine
> Et nos amours
> Faut-il qu'il m'en souvienne
> La joie venait toujours après la peine
>
> Vienne la nuit sonne l'heure
> Les jours s'en vont je demeure

Wilbur attempts to duplicate the rhyming of "Seine," "souvienne" and "peine," with this lurching monstrosity:

> Under the Mirabeau Bridge there flows the Seine
> Must I recall
> Our loves recall how then
> After each sorrow joy came back again
>
> Let night come on bells end the day
> The days go by me still I stay

Recall, recall, what the hell is "come on bells"? Are we in a Dixie diner?! Compared to Wilbur, however, Revell is even more freeflowing. Like any teenager, he confuses love with lover. The more chicks, the more deep and cheap feelings. Haight-Ashury, anyone? And water doesn't flow here but slips:

> Under Mirabeau Bridge the river slips away
>> And lovers
>> Must I be reminded
> Joy came always after pain
>> The night is a clock chiming
>> The days go by not I

Revell should have written "the river slides into first base," to make it more American. As for the Pogues, God bless them, I will not discuss their sing-along version. Enough jive already, let's go to the real jazz. Here, finally, is Reggis Tongue's extraordinary rendition:

> Under the bridge Mirabeau runs the Seine
>> And our loves
>> It is necessary that it remembers me
> The joy always came after the sorrow

>> Vienna the night sounds the hour
>> The days from go away I remain

The first thing one notices is that, unlike Wilbur, Revell and every other English translator, Meredith, Hartley, Padgett, etc, Tongue does not anglicize "le ponte Mirabeau" into "Mirabeau bridge." By not flip-flopping the French word-order, he maintains the ambiguity of "Mirabeau," which is both bridge and woman, woman as bridge, a haunting, beautiful image and the person the narrator's talking to. The "our loves" in the next line become her loves also—that's why Apollinaire writes "nos amours" and not "mes amours." Since Mirabeau denotes "Beautiful Reflection," the narrator's also talking to himself, a potential suicide seeing his face in a roiling river slip sliding away. But he does not jump, fortunately, because a mysterious "it"—God? Love? Lovers? Mirabeau, mon amour?—is reminding him that "joy always came after sorrow." The past-tense "came" maintains a tragic, suspenseful doubt, because we don't know, never will, if joy will ever come again. With the next two lines, Tongue unleashes on us the full genius of his translation prowess. He does not mechanically convert "Vienne la nuit" into "Comes the night" but, noticing the capitalized "Vienne," understands that Apollinaire is punning "vienne" with "Vienne," the capitalized capital of the Austrian-Hungarian empire. With this subtle and masterful stroke, the poet evokes Mozart's "Eine Kleine Nachtmusik," composed in Vienna in 1787. A little night music remembered, and hoped for, a bit of nookies, the joy that always came after the sorrow. Another striking musical allusion enlivens the next line. The first modern man, Apollinaire exults in pop culture: "The days from go away I remain" is a barely-concealed paraphrase of Paul Simon's "You know the nearer your destination, the more you slip sliding away." So rivers do slip away, after all. My apologies, then, to Monsieur Donald Revell.

Tom Bird

Not since the appearance and disappearance,
Let us pray, of Richard Kostelanetz have we seen
A wordsmith, or rather, word generator, this gratis.
In the mid 80's, when one couldn't gain two steps
Without mashing a Lyn Lifshin effort, Tom Bird
Debuted with his "All Lies, Especially the Truth,"
A delicate cycle of sparse, wrenching melodies
About his knotted girlhood. These "confessions"
So convinced, many readers assumed Tom Bird
To be a nom de guerre. Next came "Dragon, Gong
& Bamboo Shack," a multi-lingual audio guide into
The labyrinthian mess of the Asian-American psyche.
In it, we are told that Bruce Lee, a hard nip, is slang
For an anxious bling-bling. Then "Bluce Ree Sightings,"
"Shoah Nuff," then "The Marginalia of Steppin Fetchit."

Next came Tom's neo-geo, arctic exploration, each poem
Was constructed according to the universally acclaimed,
Timeless and possibly divine formula of the golden mean:

½ + $\sqrt{(5/4)}$ or ½ - $\sqrt{(5/4)}$

Which translate into:

1.618033988749894... or 0.618033988749894...

For variation, he also sampled Fibonacci, or fib, numbers:

0, 1, 1, 2, 3, 5, 8, 13, 21, 34, 55, 89, 144, 233...

Worn out by these mathematical poetic flexings, Bird
Rediscovered his flesh in a series of performance verses,
All with blunt photographic evidences: "Poetry Composed
In the Nude," also known as "The Panhandle Variations,"
"Poems Made with Unclean Subtances" and "Poems
Forcibly Drawn Out under Prolonged yet Legal Torture."

One Request and Five Questions

Stop torturing me, OK? I feel it, and it's torturing me.

Why do you torture me day and night? You don't even

Know me and you're torturing me? Angel, you just love

To torture people on purpose, don't you? It's obvious

That you get a serious hard-on seeing people tortured.

Is your boredom torturing you? In real life, if you're nasty

To me at all, I'm gonna make sure I fuck you up permanently,

Because I hate people who torture me, OK? That's logic.

My Local Burning

If it feels and looks like racing,
And crashes, hallelujah, like racing,
Then it's World War III all right.

Hapless, uninspired civvies of all ages
Ducking behind dumpsters. To rake them
Is less than lame, even with the massive
Ordnance up your dead mama's ass.

When this endless ride's finally history,
You can return and camp fire inside her
Ample back hatch, and stare back down
The 12-lane highway of your combustion.

Gazebos on astro lawns, incinerated firs.
These explosions are so surprisingly realistic,
When I saw my local burning, I almost cried.

Future Weapons

Our dipsticks dry—hell, we don't even
Have a dipstick, it's in the locked museum
Of seething nostalgia—we use wooden arrows.
Every man worth a cow must have an oiled bow,
Sheath, 24 straight ones and a furnished spear.

From 12 until 50, you unleashed six a day—
That's 82,992 shots!—most of them way off
The painted butt. False in aim, wobbly in flight,
Horseless man, you'll never make an archer.

"Bombing each time, it don't help me none to call
These twigs, branchlets, whatever, smart arrows.
I'm spose to be one with the freakin bull's eye.
To miss is a contradiction. Sheeeeeit."

Wussies will always shun wappenshaws,
But I can't wait until the next weapon show.

The Earliest Poetry

Digging for a new well, we discovered a weird book yesterday.
Though very heavy, it has only two pages, or rather, one page
And a sort of black mirror. The oldest man living has never seen
Or heard of such a weird book. I must be poetry, we assume,
Though we don't know what language it's in. All the lines
Are of equal length—a rigid, formalist construction. The first:

Esc F1 F2 F3 F3 F4 F5 F6 F7 F8 F9 F10 F11 F12 Num LK

It must be added that there is variety in this crude poem.
The last line has a surprising, breathtaking caesura:

Ctrl Fn [weird symbol] Alt————Alt Gr [another weird symbol]

This discovery proves that many years ago, our forefathers
Already had a taste for poetry, although their stamina
Was not great.

An Awful Joke

Check out my muscles, man, I lost 5 pounds
Chasing a pound of flesh, then I lost another pound
Killing, plucking, cleaning and grilling it. By the time
Its gizzard eased down my gullet, I was dead.

Deism Help Us

"A Chinese fellow from around here,
Goes by the name of Tong Peng, said:
'May you live in interesting times, these
Are the times that try men's souls.'"
[overheard in a Thetford pub, 21st century]

May chickens, hamsters and pigs jockey
For real estate on your ancestral roof—
Check!

May your thin, wheezing ox collapse
On the Interstate while cart-pooling—
Check!

May pesty populations
Fester in your crotches—
Check!

May your tomato cease to be tomato.
May your garlic cease to be garlic—
Check!

May your seasons blur into one. May
You never see another Super Bowl—
Check!

Metropoles

There was a city so vast, milk could not be
Delivered from its outlying farms to the center
Without turning into yogurt, sometimes cheese,
Depending on the weather.

Eroded by greed, an entire city, every skyscraper,
Shack and subdivision, would tilt 45 degrees,
Until it kissed the splattered pavement.

They built one-hundred-story towers,
Only to occupy the first three floors, the rest
Were haunted by their pissed-off ancestors.

Amid cheers and booing, drunk adventurers
Would set out for the darkened highest floors,
Never to return.

Ruins encrusted upon ruins, these dark ruins
Are organic, growing centuries by centuries, until
The lights are turned on again.

2084

Bone soap, pubic hair cigs, grass tea,
We make do with milk substitute, egg
And sperm substitute, shit substitute.

Shit, ma, ain't got shit
To eat round here, not even
Some jive shit. [haiku]

Only the barest few, buck naked, can afford nothing.

I was cleaved from my wife, kids and refrigerator,
Then cleaved from my own bones. Whew!

Beaming happy eyes around a yew tree,
Last one in the hemisphere, apparently.

What's a slipper bath? What's an 8-track player?
What's a lug wrench? What's a rearview mirror?

Recent Archeo News

20 February 3006—Ancient toilet
Discovered in Boston, lid missing.

8 February 3006—30 billion scraps
Of well-preserved, well-made plastic
Accidentally unearthed in Athens.

30 January 3006—3-foot-long
"COSMIC EXPANDING" toy sword
Excavated in outskirts of Beijing.

24 January 3006—Large glass menagerie
Recovered just off-shore, near Key West.

22 January 3006—Post-modern poem
Found in dog's grave, tucked in anus.

16 January 3006—Tattoos, salacious,
Shed light on 21st Century Tokyo.

14 January 3006—Plastic barrettes, polyester scrunchies
And rare titanium navel ring shaped like lovely butterfly
Interred with disturbed skeleton of teenaged girl.

13 January 3006—Chubby male mummy
With lots of loose change, buried erect
In well-preserved peep show cubicle.

9 January 3006—Miraculous city of Dubai
Discovered nearly intact in deserted desert.

1 January 3006—Oxidized brass
Trumpets and cornets found bobbing
In New Orleans waters.

24 December 3005—Tire tracks, chewing gum,
Bolts, pegs, screws, pins, nails and human hair
Detected in ancient asphalt driveway.

17 December 3005—Plethora of megalomaniac
And glib sculptures in corporate spaces offer
Abundant proofs that 20th century man
Was prone to lead poisoning.

15 December 3005—Nasty skull hookahs
And dead head bongs excite experts.

Cyclopian Economics

With hard cheeses generally favored, cheddar has become
A near-universal currency, with pecorino, beaufort, gouda, jack,
Appenzeller, emmental, comte and colby also widely accepted.
In the Middle East, there is an aversion towards rennet. There,

The locals make do with the crumbly, easily-depreciated feta.

Soft cheeses don't barter well, even those that age well, and
For self-evident reason, valdeon, cambozola, cabrales, brie,
Saint agur, stilton and montbriac are absolutely not fungible.

Tale from the Desert

This you must know, it is a tale of consequence:
For their water festival, the villagers of Los Angeles
Would build, out of odd bits of masonry, a huge effigy
Of a so-called English toilet. Elected W.C. Queen,

A large virgin would perch on this while everyone
Make hydraulic, irrigating noises, while chanting:
"Crapping in fresh water! Crapping in fresh water!"

They also make violent throwing motions, as if
Stoning her to death.

Hibernation 101

First, maintenance and tune-up work on ambulance,
Then solid, reliable citizen's band radio purchased.
Before corpse of client, freshly dead, could be whisked
From solemn thatched cottage, ice must be purchased.
Contract stipulates that undersigned be kept super cool
For long as it takes for science to catch up with death.

Beloved Alone

Standing in deep snow, don't look forward to the late bus
Swinging around the corner, at last, don't look forward to Friday,
5 o'clock or the end of your unjust sentence, don't look forward
To the landing of this numbing, trans-everything flight, thank you
For your patience, don't look forward to the return of your Daddy,
Because, for every second of each long day, you must remember
What DaVinci said: "A man who looks forward to Spring
Is looking forward to his own death."

About Linh Dinh

Linh Dinh was born in Saigon, Vietnam in 1963, came to the US in 1975, and has also lived in Italy and England. He is the author of two collections of stories, *Fake House* (Seven Stories Press 2000) and *Blood and Soap* (Seven Stories Press 2004), and three previous books of poems, *All Around What Empties Out* (Tinfish 2003), *American Tatts* (Chax 2005) and *Borderless Bodies* (Factory School 2006) . His work has been anthologized in *Best American Poetry 2000, Best American Poetry 2004, Best American Poetry 2007* and *Great American Prose Poems from Poe to the Present*, among other places. Linh Dinh is also the editor of the anthologies *Night, Again: Contemporary Fiction from Vietnam* (Seven Stories Press 1996) and *Three Vietnamese Poets* (Tinfish 2001), and translator of *Night, Fish and Charlie Parker*, the poetry of Phan Nhien Hao (Tupelo 2006). *Blood and Soap* was chosen by the Village Voice as one of the best books of 2004. His poems and stories have been translated into Italian, Spanish, German, Porguese, Japanese, and Arabic. He has also published widely in Vietnamese.

Recent Books from Chax Press

Waterwork, by Sarah Riggs

Since I Moved In, by Tim Peterson

Begin at Once, by Beth Joselow

Mirth, by Linda Russo

Swoon Noir, by Bruce Andrews

Witness, by Kathleen Fraser and Nancy Tokar Miller (limited fine art edition)

Under Virga, by Joe Amato

Afterimage, by Charles Borkhuis

Analects on a Chinese Screen, by Glenn Mott

Sentimental Blue, by Jefferson Carter

American Tatts, by Linh Dinh

Accidental Species, by Kass Fleisher

Hostile, by Heather Nagami

Black Valentine, by David Abel

Deaccessioned Landscapes, by Jonathan Brannen

A-Reading Spicer and 18 Sonnets, by Beverly Dahlen

Erased Art, by Tenney Nathanson

Chantry, by Elizabeth Treadwell

Born Two, by Allison Cobb

A Book of Concealments, by Jerome Rothenberg

Hegelian Honeymoon, by Nick Piombino

For more information, please see our web site: http://www.chax.org

Chax Press is supported by the Tucson Pima Arts Council, and by the Arizona Commission on the Arts, with funding from the State of Arizona and the National Endowment for the Arts.